NATIONAL FOOTBALL LEAGUE

POWER PLAYERS

by Paul Ladewski

SCHOLASTIC INC.

New York   Toronto   London   Auckland   Sydney
Mexico City   New Delhi   Hong Kong   Buenos Aires

All photos © **Getty Images**.

Front cover (left to right): Steve Dykes; Jonathan Daniel; Harry How

Back Cover (left to right): Jim McIsaac; Andy Lyons; Jonathan Daniel

Interior: Title page (clockwise from left): Elsa; Elsa; Jed Jacobsohn; Doug Pensinger; Ronald Martinez; (3) Donald Miralle; (4, 14, 23) Elsa; (5) Al Messerschmidt; (6) Scott Boehm; (7) Gregory Shamus; (8, 12, 31, 32 right) Jonathan Daniel; (9) Rick Stewart; (10) Sam Greenwood; (11) Otto Greule Jr; (13, 25) Andy Lyons; (15) Steve Dykes; (16, 22) Doug Pensinger; (17, 18, 24) Jim McIsaac; (19) Chris Graythen; (20) Ronald Martinez; (21) Matthew Stockman; (26) Jed Jacobsohn; (27) Stephen Dunn; (28) Doug Benc; (29) Greg Trott; (30) Nick Laham; (32 left) Harry How

ISBN-13: 978-0-545-06545-0
ISBN-10: 0-545-06545-3

Published by Scholastic Inc.
SCHOLASTIC and associated logos are trademarks and/or registered trademarks of Scholastic Inc.

12 11 10 9 8 7 6 5 4 3   8/0

Designed by Cheung Tai
Printed in the U.S.A.
First Scholastic printing, August 2008

TOM BRADY

TOM BRADY

Many consider New England Patriots quarterback Tom Brady to be the best in football, but the road to the top wasn't a smooth one.

At Michigan, Tom began his college career as the seventh quarterback on the team. It frustrated him to sit on the bench. At one point, he even thought about a move to another school.

In his final two seasons, Tom got a chance to be the starter, and the Wolverines won 20 of 25 games. No matter. Several NFL scouts doubted whether he was physically strong enough to play at the next level.

Sure enough, on the weekend of the 2000 draft, Tom waited and waited and waited for his name to be called. At last, the Patriots chose him in the sixth round. Tom was the 199th player to be selected.

Tom started his first season as the team's fourth position quarterback. Before the season was over, however, the rookie had worked his way up to the second position. Even so, he only threw three passes the entire season.

After the starting Patriots quarterback went down with an injury, Tom got his chance to show his stuff, and he hasn't stopped. He led the "Brady Bunch" to three Super Bowl victories and was selected Most Valuable Player in two of them.

"One thing about Tom is, he's smart and prepares very hard," says Bill Belichick, his head coach. "Pressure doesn't really bother him."

In the 2007–8 season Tom was terrific. In fact, he was better than any QB had ever been. Tom threw a record 50 touchdowns and led his team to an 18–1 record, only losing in the final game of the year: the Super Bowl.

Sometimes it's not how fast you run or how far you throw that counts most. As Tom proves, sometimes it's how well you think the game and how badly you want to succeed that matters more than anything.

DREW BREES

DREW BREES

After Hurricane Katrina blew through the New Orleans area two years ago, many people wondered if it would be possible to pick up the pieces. The New Orleans Saints, led by their star quarterback Drew Brees, were determined to help.

Drew spent a lot of time and energy working to help the city, so much so that he was selected NFL Man of the Year for his efforts. In his first season with the team, he also led the Saints to the playoffs for one of the few times in their history, giving Saints fans hope for the future.

Months later, New Orleans is still in need of help. Because Hurricane Katrina is old news, however, there are fewer volunteers and donations now. But that won't stop Drew.

"I was brought here for a reason," he says. "I feel like I can make a tremendous impact, not only with the team, but in the community."

At 6 feet, 209 pounds, Drew isn't the tallest or the fastest or the strongest quarterback in the league. But as the folks in New Orleans will tell you, he's definitely one of the toughest around.

"This city and I — we have some similarities," says Drew, who signed with the Saints after a serious shoulder problem had left his career in doubt. "A lot of people think we may not come back."

Last season, Drew set about proving the doubters wrong by putting up big numbers across the board. He completed nearly two passes for every three pass attempts. He averaged 276.4 yards in the air per game. He fired 28 touchdowns.

Because of their success the previous season, however, the Saints were no longer a surprise to their opponents. With injuries forcing some of their best players to sit out, the team finished with an 7–9 record and watched the playoffs on television.

But like the city they represent, the Saints have some unfinished business on their hands. And Drew won't be content until it gets done. Just as New Orleans refused to quit on him, Drew won't quit on New Orleans.

BRAYLON EDWARDS

BRAYLON EDWARDS

At 6-foot-3 and weighing 212 pounds, Cleveland Browns star Braylon Edwards is an unusual package of flash and dash at the wide receiver position.

Braylon makes so many amazing catches that it seems like he has Velcro on his hands sometimes. Additionally, the former Michigan star has the physical strength to run over defensive backs, and the speed to blow past them as well.

In 2007, the Browns were one of the surprise teams in the league. As for Braylon, he caught 80 balls for 1,289 yards and 16 touchdowns. New England Patriots star Randy Moss was the only player at the position to score more times.

The Browns selected Braylon at the third pick in the 2005 NFL draft, but because of injuries, he got off to a slow start. As a rookie, he sat out two games because of an infection. A torn ligament in his right knee cut his second season short.

Now that Braylon feels good again, he has even bigger plans for the future. A trip to the playoffs is at the top of his to-do list.

Yet while Braylon is a Pro Bowl receiver on the field, what makes the 25-year-old even more special is how much he wants to be a giver off it.

Last year Braylon donated $1 million to Cleveland public schools. The money was used to help 100 eighth-graders afford college educations. In order to be eligible for one of the $10,000 gifts, students had to have at least a 2.5 grade-point average, perform 15 hours of community service, and attend workshops.

"Kids deal with so much outside of school, sometimes they don't have a reason to come to school," explains Braylon. "That's not an excuse for not coming to school, but they need support. We all have a duty to help."

He also wants to raise money, and get businesses and education groups involved so that more needy kids will stay in school.

Like the touchdown Braylon scored against the Cincinnati Bengals early last season, when he made a diving catch then rolled into the end zone before he was touched, this guy isn't one to quit until he reaches his goal.

DAVID GARRARD

DAVID GARRARD

I n his first full season as a starter, quarterback David Garrard (pronounced guh-RARD) threw for 18 touchdowns and led the Jacksonville Jaguars to the second round of the playoffs.

But David isn't just about touchdowns and playoff invitations. His story is also about patience, loyalty, and hard work.

David set all kinds of records at East Carolina, where he attended college, so when the Jaguars selected him in the fourth round of the 2002 NFL draft almost everybody thought he would be their number one quarterback soon. After all, David had a powerful, accurate arm, and strong legs and quick feet which gave him options on the field, but then the Jaguars drafted another QB before the 2003 season, and David spent more time on the bench. Rather than slacking off, however, he continued to work hard on the practice field and study off it.

In January 2004, David began to experience severe stomach pains. Tests revealed that he had Crohn's disease, which is painful but treatable. In a matter of weeks, he lost nearly 40 pounds. David underwent surgery to remove a portion of his swollen intestines, but he was back on the field one month later.

"It's a horrible disease, something that a lot of people are affected by," David says. "But I think the Lord blessed me with it, so I could talk about it."

David got a chance to play after the starting quarterback was injured midway through the 2004 season. He could have signed with another team after the season was over, but he decided to stay put.

He kept working, using his time on the bench to learn as much as he could. Finally, he won the top job before the start of the 2007 season, his sixth in the league, and he didn't let go of it.

"Things worked out for the best, didn't they?" asks David, even though he already knows the answer.

Then again, if anybody can turn a negative into a positive, David is the guy.

DEVIN HESTER

DEVIN HESTER

Want to start a friendly debate? Then ask your pals "Who is the fastest player in the NFL?"

Because there are so many fleet feet in the league, nobody knows the answer for sure. But if you cast your vote for Devin Hester, the Chicago Bears' human blur, then it's hard for anyone to argue with you.

At 5-foot-11, 189 pounds, Devin is the Roadrunner among so many Wile E. Coyotes on the field. At Suncoast High School in Riviera Beach, Florida, he was clocked at 4.33 in the 40-yard dash. Before the 2006 NFL draft, Devin improved his time to 4.27 at the same distance.

"I want to show the world that I run a 4.3 and could slip into a 4.2," Devin says.

What makes Devin such a threat to score any time he touches the ball is his ability to dart through a hole quickly. Once he gets in the open field, it's see ya' later, buddy.

But Devin is more than a one-trick pony. While it's easy to be blinded by his speed, the man known as the Windy City Flyer also has strong legs that allow him to run through a defender when necessary. On many of his touchdown scampers, Devin breaks at least one tackle along the way.

While Devin may or may not be the fastest player these days, he certainly is the best kick returner around. In fact, he may be the best *ever*.

Last season, Devin carried back six kicks for touchdowns to break the league record, which he had set as a rookie the previous year. He needs only two more TDs to become the all-time leader—and he's only 25 years old!

Like it or not, defenses will probably see even more of Devin in the years to come.

Devin lined up at wide receiver for the first time last season. Because he had played defensive back in college, the new position was not easy to learn. But as the season moved along, Devin got better. He caught 20 balls, two of them for touchdowns.

"I just want to be a key player," Devin says. "Whenever I'm called on, I just want to make the play at the right time. I want to step up and do my best."

RANDY MOSS

RANDY MOSS

There are a few wide receivers who are faster than a speeding bullet, more powerful than a locomotive, and able to leap over tall defenders in a single bound. But there is only one who is just plain super: Randy Moss of the New England Patriots.

In the 2007 season, Randy caught 23 touchdowns passes, more than any player in NFL history. The record-setting touchdown took place in late December, when the Patriots beat the New York Giants to complete a perfect 16-0 regular season. And it came on quarterback Tom Brady's record-setting fiftieth touchdown pass.

Randy finished the season with 98 catches and 1,493 yards. One of Brady's favorite targets was reached: he didn't fumble the ball once.

"At any given time, our offense can move up and down the field," Randy says. "We've got [an amazing] offensive line and a great quarterback. It's up to us to make it happen. We can give anyone the ball and move it up the field."

Nobody can move quite like Randy, though. He's a 6-foot-4, 210-pound package of flash and dash.

"Randy is the best receiver in the league," says Giants receiver Plaxico Burress, who's not too shabby himself.

Randy was born on February 13, 1977, in Rand, West Virginia, a small town near Charleston. He was raised by his mother, Maxine, who worked as a nurse's aide.

At DuPont High School, it didn't take long to notice that Randy was a different kind of athlete than the rest of the kids. He ran the 40-yard dash in 4.25 seconds. In the vertical jump, he was measured at 39 inches.

Randy was also excellent in baseball and track, but he stood out in basketball and football especially. He was named West Virginia Player of the Year in basketball twice and in football once. He decided to play football at Marshall, where he attended college.

Ten years later, it's safe to say that Randy made the right choice.

ADRIAN PETERSON

ADRIAN PETERSON

Before last season, no NFL player had ever run for more than 295 yards in one game.

Of course, the league hadn't seen many players quite like Adrian Peterson, the Minnesota Vikings rookie who burst out of nowhere like some sort of human Halley's Comet last season.

A rare blend of speed, strength, and quickness, Adrian exploded for a record 296 yards versus the San Diego Chargers in only the eighth game of his career. Three weeks earlier, he bolted for 224 yards in a victory against the Chicago Bears.

"Sometimes I sit back and think, 'Is this really happening?'" says Adrian, who stands 6-foot-1, weighs 217 pounds and is known as A.D. because he can run All Day long.

Adrian finished the season with 1,341 yards on the ground, more than any player except LaDainian Tomlinson, the Chargers' star back. As a result, he was the runaway choice for Rookie Offensive Player of the Year.

And get this: Adrian didn't start his first game until the sixth week of the season!

How does he do it?

"I run to daylight when I see an opening," says the former Oklahoma star, not quite sure himself.

Actually, Adrian doesn't just run to daylight. He sprints to it. When an opponent does get a hand on him, he has the strength to shrug it off.

For this, Adrian can thank his genes. His mother, Bonita Jackson, was a track and field star at the University of Houston. His father, Nelson, played basketball at Idaho State. And his uncle, Ivory Lee Brown, was an NFL player.

Only injury can stop Adrian, it seems.

Late in the 2007 season, Adrian sprained his right knee and had to sit out two games. Who knows what he might have accomplished without that enforced break?

If A.D. stays healthy, many predict that he'll run and run and run some more until he reaches the Hall of Fame one day.

BEN ROETHLISBERGER

From his arm to his name to his accomplishments, almost everything about Pittsburgh Steelers quarterback Ben Roethlisberger is big.

In 2004, Big Ben led the Steelers to 13 straight wins, a record for a rookie quarterback. One year later, at only 23 years of age, he became the youngest QB to win a Super Bowl. Last season, Big Ben had the most touchdown throws (32) and highest passer rating (104.1) in team history.

"I'm not a guy who's going to be yelling or ranting and raving and trying to talk to be a leader," says Big Ben, who checks in at 6-foot-5, 241 pounds. "I'd rather lead by example. It has made me feel more comfortable out there on the field."

Then again, Big Ben has plenty of motivation to do well each week.

Hey, how would you like to have to look Zeus and Hercules in the eyes after a loss?

Zeus, a Rotweiler, and Hercules, a Bernese Mountain Dog, are Big Ben's roommates.

"I am assuming it would be like two brothers," Big Ben says of their relationship. "They are fighting in the back seat of the car, and Zeus pulls my other dog's tail. It is comical at times. Makes life pretty enjoyable at my house."

Big Ben is such a big animal lover that he donates a service dog to a local police department in the cities where the Steelers play each season. He decided to step forward after one named Flip the Wonder Dog was shot and killed in his hometown two years ago.

"My dad instilled in me a love and respect for animals," says Big Ben, who starred at Miami University in Ohio. "This is a good way to combine that passion with a desire to support the police and fire departments."

On the field, Big Ben reminds many of former Denver Broncos star John Elway, the quarterback he admired most as a kid.

Like John, Big Ben has a rocket right arm, strong legs, and nimble feet. Also like John, he wears number 7 on his jersey.

Yet more than football makes Big Ben tick inside. As Zeus and Hercules would tell you if they could, he's a doggone good guy, too.

TONY ROMO

TONY ROMO

Dallas Cowboys quarterback Tony Romo is proof that, with a lot of practice and a little bit of luck, dreams can come true.

Born on April 21, 1980, Tony grew up in Wisconsin. There he attended Burlington High School and idolized Brett Favre, the Green Bay Packers star quarterback. Tony was a QB himself, but his team lost more games than it won in his final two seasons.

The major colleges had no interest in Tony as a football player, so he chose Eastern Illinois instead. Even though he was selected for the Walter Payton Award as the top Division 1-AA player in the country, his name wasn't called in the NFL draft a few months later.

Finally, in 2003, the Cowboys signed Tony to be their third-string quarterback. When Tony got a chance to start his first professional game two years later, he led the team to a victory against the Carolina Panthers.

And Tony hasn't stopped since then.

"There comes a point in the game when you got to make a play or you got to do something to get your team over the hump," explains Tony, who likes to play golf and listen to rock music in his spare time. "When time comes, you got to be able to do it."

What makes Tony so dangerous is his ability to make plays in many ways.

At 6-foot-2, Tony is tall enough to see his receivers downfield. He also moves very well, which gives them more time to get open. Tony can throw sidearm or even underhanded and still hit the target.

Last season, Tony threw for 300 yards or more in seven games. He also set team records for the most completions (335), yards (4,211), and touchdown passes (36) in one season. Even better, he guided the team to a 13-3 record and an NFC playoff berth.

Now Tony and the 'Boys have one more dream to live—a Super Bowl championship.

LADAINIAN TOMLINSON

LADAINIAN TOMLINSON

San Diego Chargers superstar LaDainian Tomlinson wants to be judged not only by his performance on the field, but also what he does *off* the field.

As much as LaDainian produces on the field—he scored a record 31 touchdowns in the 2006 season—few, if any, professional athletes give back more after the final whistle.

After wildfires blazed through Southern California last fall, LaDainian helped organize a public tribute as a way to say thank you to those who saved lives and protected homes in dangerous conditions.

"People think athletes are the real heroes, but all we do is entertain and try to set the right example for people." LaDainian told the crowd. "The firefighters, the sheriffs, the nurses, the doctors—you guys are the real heroes, because you're protecting us and keeping us safe."

In addition to events like that one, LaDainian tries to help the community year round. For example, each year he provides food for families to prepare Thanksgiving dinners. He hands out bikes and shoes to needy kids in the San Diego area, passes out gifts and encourages patients at local hospitals.

In the summer, LaDainian has his own charity golf tournament, which raises money for college scholarships. L.T. also sponsors camps for needy children in San Diego and Fort Worth, Texas, where he attended college.

During the season, LaDainian buys tickets for 21—21 is his uniform number—kids to attend Chargers home games. After the game, he shakes hands, signs autographs, and poses for pictures with them.

"People may remember something I did on the field for a couple of days, maybe a week," LaDainian will tell you. "But the things that I do and we do in the community are something that people remember for the rest of their lives."

Because of sprained ligaments in his right knee, LaDainian didn't match his numbers of the previous season, when he set a bunch of records. Even so, he ran for 1,474 yards, the most in the league. He also scored 18 touchdowns.

OSI UMENYIORA

OSI UMENYIORA

One thousand one, one thousand two, one thousand three . . .

That's usually how long it takes New York Giants defensive end Osi Umenyiora to get to the quarterback. Or about as long as it takes some people to say his name.

Osi is pronounced OH-see. Umenyiora is pronounced Yoo-men-YUR-ah. No matter how you say his name, though, Osi spells T-R-O-U-B-L-E for the player with the ball in his hands.

The surest way to stop the pass is to put heat on the quarterback, and Osi does this as well as anyone. At 6-foot-3, 261 pounds, he has the speed to blow past an offensive lineman. And Osi has the size and strength to bowl over one or even two blockers on his way to the backfield.

"You just focus on the guy in front of you, then you look up," Osi says of his secret. "Usually when you look up, you get the quarterback."

Osi was born in London to Nigerian parents. His family moved to Nigeria, then to Alabama. It wasn't until Osi was nine years old that he began to play football, but when he did, he caught on quickly. In his final year at Troy University, which is located in Alabama, his 16 sacks were second in the nation.

Selected in the second round of the 2003 NFL draft, Osi started to make a name for himself. Two years later, he had 14 1/2 sacks and was selected to play in the Pro Bowl for the first time.

In one game last season, Osi set a team record with six sacks. A few weeks later, he tackled the quarterback, caused a fumble, picked up the ball, and returned it for a touchdown—all on the same play! He finished the season with 13 sacks, five forced fumbles, and was a Pro Bowler once again.

The Giants defense played like giants in Super Bowl XLII, and Osi stood as tall as anyone on the field. His biggest play took place in the final minute before halftime, when he fell on a loose ball to stop a drive.

REGGIE WAYNE

REGGIE WAYNE

The grass looks greener on the other side, they say, but it's a wise person who understands that it probably has rocks and weeds like everywhere else.

Just ask Indianapolis wide receiver Reggie Wayne, who along with Marvin Harrison, forms one of the best twosomes in football. As a future Hall of Famer, Marvin caught most of the balls and got most of the attention.

"If you ask me, I never get enough balls," Reggie jokes. "But at the same time, I'm blessed with a lot of talent around me and a lot that can make big plays. It's one of those things around here that you pick your poison."

Even though Reggie was frustrated at times, there were a lot worse places for him to be, he figured.

After all, the Colts were one of the best teams in the league. In Peyton Manning, they had one of the best quarterbacks around.

So rather than hang his head, Reggie learned from Marvin and worked hard on his game. Sure enough, he improved every season. After 27 pass receptions as a rookie, his totals zoomed up. 49 . . . 68 . . . 77 . . . 83 . . . 86, finally hitting 104 last season.

The 2006 season was a memorable one for Reggie and his team. In Super Bowl XLI, he grabbed a 53-yard touchdown pass as the Colts won it all. A few days later, he played in the Pro Bowl for the first time in his career.

"Whenever you win in this league, it's fun," says Reggie, who played his college ball at the University of Miami in Florida. "But our opponents are probably getting sick of it."

When Marvin was slowed by a knee problem last season, Reggie was ready and able to take over as the main man. He scored 10 touchdowns and was a Pro Bowler once again.

As far as Reggie is concerned, the grass looks just fine where he is, thank you very much.

MARIO WILLIAMS

MARIO WILLIAMS

Houston Texans defensive end Mario Williams is a man with many hobbies. He likes to play video games in his spare time. He also chills out with his remote control cars and helicoptor.

Then there's his favorite pastime of all—chasing down quarterbacks every autumn.

Super Mario hauled down 14 passers in 2007, his second season in the league. Only two players had more sacks. The tall Texan also had 59 tackles.

Mario proved a lot of people wrong while he did it, too.

In 2006, Houston selected Mario at the first pick of the draft. Many Texan fans were angry when they heard the announcement. They wanted Reggie Bush, the former USC star who had won the Heisman Trophy a few weeks earlier, or quarterback Vince Young, whose Texas team beat USC in the national championship game.

What some people forgot was that, while Reggie and Vince are phenomenal athletes, Mario is no slo-mo himself. Before the draft, the former North Carolina State star was timed at 4.66 in the 40-yard dash. He also had a 40 $\frac{1}{2}$-inch vertical jump. And Mario stands 6-foot-7 and weighs 291 pounds!

No matter. While Reggie and Vince opened eyes in their first seasons, Mario failed to live up to expectations, partly because of a sore left foot. Even though the kid was only 21 years old, some considered him to be a flop already.

Mario wasted no time turning the boos to cheers last season, though. In the first week, he had five tackles, two sacks, and returned a fumble for a touchdown. Mario had 2 $\frac{1}{2}$ sacks in a game against Vince and the Tennessee Titans a few weeks later.

"It's not like a get-back thing," Mario says. "I just go out and try to play ball."

Mario was disappointed not to be invited to the Pro Bowl after the season, but he'll be more motivated than ever now.

Better watch your backs, QBs.

PATRICK WILLIS

PATRICK WILLIS

How do you find San Francisco 49ers star linebacker Patrick Willis on a football field? Simple. Just follow the ball, because number 52 in the red and gold uniform is sure to be close to it.

Clocking at 4.51 in the 40-yard dash, Patrick is fast. And at 6-foot-1, 242 pounds, he is tough. In his first season, Patrick led the league with 174 tackles, which was 33 more than the next highest total.

Is it any surprise that Patrick was selected Defensive Rookie of the Year?

"A lot of great players have won this honor," Patrick says. "I am thankful for the support I have received from my parents, my teammates, and my coaches in getting through some tough times."

Indeed, if Patrick knows how to deliver hard hits, then maybe it's because he took so many himself early in his life.

Patrick was 4 years old when his parents separated. Six years later, he worked in a cotton field to earn money for his family. In high school, Patrick, his brother, and two sisters were neglected by their father, so his basketball coach became his legal guardian. When Patrick was 21, his youngest brother, Detris, drowned.

"I've been through a tough road," Patrick says. "But I know that, no matter what, if someone knocks you down, you have to find a way to get up and get the job done. That's what you have to do."

At tiny Central High School in Bruceton, Tennessee, Patrick was named Class A Mr. Football in the state. He attended the University of Mississippi and became a starter in his junior year. That season Patrick played with a torn knee ligament, a separated shoulder, a broken finger, and a broken foot—and he still led the country with 90 solo tackles!

When Patrick was a senior, he had 137 tackles and 11 1/2 sacks, and was named the Southeastern Conference Defensive Player of the Year. He also was selected for the Butkus Award, which is given to the top linebacker in the country each year.

Now, two years later, nothing could be finer than to be this 49er.

BRETT FAVRE

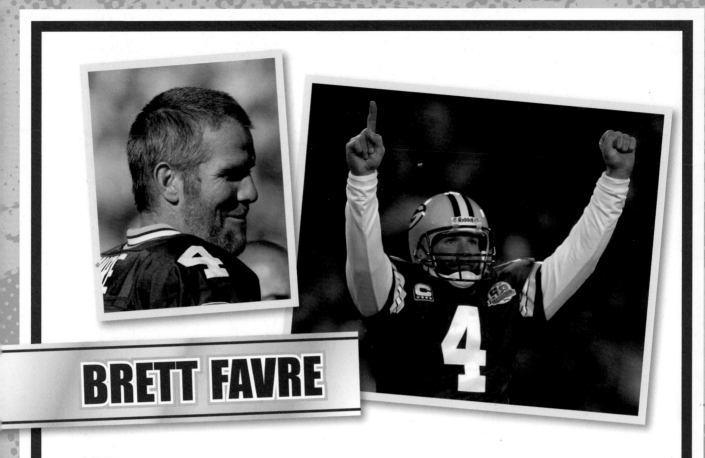

BRETT FAVRE

For seventeen seasons, Green Bay's Brett Favre was the happiest "kid" in the NFL. He tossed spirals—and snowballs. He scampered around the frozen field at Lambeau and dared other teams to catch him.

At 38 years old, most football players have retired to play golf, cut the grass, and watch their kids grow up. But Brett kept on playing. In fact, he played so well that he threw 28 touchdown passes and had one of his best seasons ever. The Packers were not supposed to be a playoff contender, but Brett helped them become one of the biggest surprise stories of the 2007 season, leading them to the NFC Championship Game.

But finally, even Brett decided that enough was enough, and, in March 2008, he retired. What did he leave behind? A whole lot of memories . . . and a whole lot of records!

In his 17-year career, Brett has been selected Most Valuable Player a record three times. In addition, he has more pass completions (5,377), yards (61,655), and touchdowns (442) than any quarterback in league history.

Brett won more games (160) than anyone at his position. But the record he is most proud of is the all-time mark for consecutive starts by a quarterback (275). Since making his first career start for the Packers in 1992, he never missed a single game!

Whatever the future holds for Brett, there's one place he better count on being: Canton, Ohio, because this Packer is going to be in the Hall of Fame. And there is no doubt about that – just as there's no doubt that football fans all over the country are going to miss the sight of him playing on the snowy field at Green Bay next season.